★★★★ *MULLING ABOUT ACTING IN THE WORLD-AS-IT-IS* ★★★★

ACTION CREATES PUBLIC LIFE

Edward T. Chambers

ACTION CREATES PUBLIC LIFE
by Edward T. Chambers

Edited by Gregory F. Augustine Pierce
Cover and text design and typesetting by Patricia A. Lynch

Copyright © 2010 by Edward T. Chambers

Portions of this book were previously published in *Being Triggers Action*.

Published by ACTA Publications, 4848 N. Clark St., Chicago, IL 60640, (800) 397-2282, www.actapublications.com

All rights reserved. No part of this publication may be reproduced or transmitted in any form or by any means, electronic or mechanical, including photocopying and recording, or by any information storage and retrieval system, including the Internet, without permission from the publisher. Permission is hereby given to use short excerpts or pieces of art with proper citation in reviews and marketing copy, free bulletins, newsletters and handouts, and scholarly papers.

ISBN: 978-0-87946-426-4
Printed in the United States of America by Total Printing Systems
Year 20 19 18 17
Printing 15 14 13 12 11 10 9 8 7 6 5 4 3 2

♻ Text printed on 30% post-consumer recycled paper

A NOTE FROM THE PUBLISHER

★★★★

Ed Chambers has been organizing people for power for over fifty-five years, almost forty of them as the executive director of the Industrial Areas Foundation (IAF).

This is the fourth in Ed Chambers' series of short books on "Mulling About Acting in the World-As-It-Is." The others are *The Body Trumps the Brain*, *The Power of Relational Action*, and *Being Triggers Action*.

For those who never met Chambers, as well as for those of us who have learned much from him, these books offer an insight into the unique thinking of a man who has spent a lifetime of action in Public life. So, please enjoy *Action Creates Public Life*.

> Gregory F. Augustine Pierce
> Publisher
> ACTA Publications

INTRODUCTION

★★★★

MULLING ABOUT ACTING IN THE WORLD-AS-IT-IS

mull: 1. to study or ruminate; ponder. 2. to think about carefully; consider.

> *Webster's Encyclopedic Unabridged*
> *Dictionary of the English Language*

★★★★

To successfully make the jump from private life (that is, the world into which we were born and spend the first 15-18 years of our lives) —to Public life (which is life outside family and friends, the world of business and politics, health care and the arts, education and religion), we need to learn to act in a different way. This action is what informs, drives, and makes meaningful our Public life.

Public life is not closed and limited, the way private life is. Public life is unlimited and wide open, but we must act in such a way that we make it real and fulfilling for ourselves. It is amazing to me how many people are not able to make this jump. They can't and they don't because they haven't been taught why or how they need to act, and act differently, in Public life. (I will capitalize

"Public" life throughout this book to remind us that it is a specific kind of action that we are talking about.)

When we act in Public life, there is always and inevitably a reaction. That reaction forms the basis for our next actions. Many times, in fact, we are acting as a result of a reaction that we were actually trying to provoke by our action.

It is easier for human beings to stay in private life. Private life is the arena of our family of origin, where love is unconditional, we only deal with friends and family, and tension and conflict is supposed to be minimized. Public life is full of tension and conflict. In private life, what matters is whether or not we are accepted and liked. In Public life, it is only important that we are recognized and respected.

> **In Public life, it is only important that we are recognized and respected.**

But friends and family are not the total world. As we get older, even when we are still kids, this begins to dawn on us. "Don't walk on that lady's lawn," we are told by our parents. "She'll call the police on you." Or, "We are going to move to Milwaukee because Daddy is getting transferred by his company." Or, "Just put up with your teacher until the end of the year. Next year you will have a really nice teacher."

We begin to realize, even at a young age, that there is another whole world out there that operates very differently from what we had initially been led to believe. Everybody does not love us, everyone is not to be treated as if they were one of the family, and—here is the big one that does not really occur to us until we are teenagers—life is *not* fair! There is another life that we have to learn to operate in, and it is not like the life we have had up until that time. This is Public life.

Our immediate reaction is that it would just be easier to stay in private life, and that is the way it should be for the first 15-18 years of our life. The problem is that those who have helped us learn the lessons of private life: our parents, our grandparents and aunts and uncles, our teachers, our clergy—all the adults who care about us—don't want to prepare us for Public life. They want to protect us from it, to keep us as children as long as possible, to convince us that private life is the most important life, that "family is all that matters," that there is "nothing you can do" about the way the world is and the only thing we need worry about is getting a job and raising a family of our own. Our parents raise us, give us advice, make sure we have the basic tools of education, but they do not push us or teach us how to act in Public life. Just the opposite, they try to protect us from it, because they are afraid we might hurt ourselves or choose the "wrong" things.

The truth, of course, is just the opposite. We get about 15-18 years to "grow up" (some of us less, a few of us more), and then we are thrust into Public life—

whether we want it or not, whether we are prepared or not. Basically after high school, we are expected to either go to college or get a job or enter military service. Eventually we are all expected to decide on a career, get married or at least live with another adult person, have children and raise them, make money, get a home and a car, participate in community and political affairs, join a church or synagogue or mosque or temple, and—this is the biggest surprise of all—help make the world a better place. That is what Public life is all about, and nobody can, will, or should do it for us. We either learn to do it for ourselves or we don't.

> **We get about 15-18 years to "grow up" (some of us less, a few of us more), and then we are thrust into Public life— whether we want it or not, whether we are prepared or not.**

So we need to act in Public life, but how do we learn to do so effectively? For the most part, we are clearly not trained to do so. With some few exceptions, our educational system, our religious institutions, even our parents want to keep us like children for as long as possible, and some of us actually buy into this. But most of us are thrust into Public life, ready or not, and we have to learn how to deal with it on the fly. But there is another way. I call it "training for Public life," and it is what the Industrial Areas Foundation (IAF) has been about for the past 70 years.

We teach that all of us have got to go out into the world and make things happen. "Making things happen" is another definition of the word *action*. In the process of taking action, we meet some people we like and others we don't like, much less agree with or care about. But in Public life, the task is to get into relationship with others and see if we have enough in common to act together on the world we all share.

In Public life, everything is out there—good, bad, evil, excellence, banality, creativity, passion, apathy, saints, sinners. Action is totally about the world-as-it-is, not the world-as-we-want-it-to-be. It is the arena of the art of the possible, the world of compromise, the world of half-a-loaf-is-better-than-none.

Real action, therefore, creates Public life. We are not made to be private beings living in our isolated private worlds. We are meant to get out into the world and make our mark on it, along with other beings who are trying to do the same thing.

The world is out there, and we have to decide whether we accept it the way it is or want to change it, and if we want to change it we have to decide what we have to do and then do it. That is the ultimate purpose of Public life.

Parents pump their kids with all kinds of private-life stuff: "be nice," "get along," "don't rock the boat," "don't stand out," "don't create tension," "do what we and your teachers and your ministers tell you."

That is not what we are going to talk about here. We are going to reflect on why and how we take action in Public life. It takes a whole different way of thinking. It is about power: how we get it and how we exercise it. It is about Public relationships with one another and with those who are in power. Ultimately, it takes organization.

Most people have worked out some sort of private life for themselves, and they think that their private life is what is important. But Public life is in many ways even more important than our private lives, for it is in Public life that we find the mission or purpose that has been given to us by our creator. It is the arena of freedom, initiation, growth, collegiality. It is, in fact, adulthood. We need private life to prepare us for Public life, and if it doesn't it implodes on itself. But Public life is the broader arena. We have to move out of our childhood patterns in order to find out who we really are *in relationship to others* and *in relationship to the world*. In so doing, we will act, rather than react, to the world-as-it-is.

Most people do not even find their spouse in their private life. They have to go out into the world and find someone who is not exactly like them in order to form a new family, create children, and build a new private life away from the private life in which they were raised. And even then, both husband and wife must have a full

Public life outside the home if they are to have a healthy relationship and if their children are to have healthy role models.

If we could grow up in ten days, we probably wouldn't even need private life at all. We need private life to prepare us for Public life. But we absolutely need Public life if we are to fulfill our potential as human beings. In fact, Public life is more important than private life. You can have a bad private life and still have a great Public life. The problem for most people is that they do not have much of a Public life at all, and this puts too much pressure on their private life.

> **We absolutely need Public life if we are to fulfill our potential as human beings.**

So, this book is about how to develop a good, strong, adult Public life. To get a fulfilling Public life, we have to know how to act and how to act effectively.

Edward T. Chambers
Chicago, Illinois
2010

ACTION CREATES PUBLIC LIFE

★★★★

*A life of reaction is a life of slavery,
intellectually and spiritually.
One must fight for a life of action, not reaction.*

Rita Mae Brown (civil rights leader)

★★★★

Allow me to get philosophical for a moment. When we talk about "action," what are we really talking about? The word "act" comes from the Greek word *agein*, which means to "do, drive, lead." So, even though our English verb to act is an intransitive verb, it has the connotation of driving or leading something or someone. In fact, the very first definition of the noun act in *Webster's Unabridged International Dictionary* of the English Language is "the exertion of power."

In physics, "power" is defined as "force times distance, divided by time." What does this mean for our action in the world-as-it-is?

The first thing this definition means is that life must struggle with the resistance of inert matter. This is why power requires "force," or effort and energy. This understanding of the physical nature of the world is something that I only came to understand and appreciate older in life. When we are young, no task is too daunting. We think we can do anything we set our minds to. Perhaps that is why Jesus said we had to "become like children" if we were going to build the kingdom of God "on earth as it is in heaven." Every parent of young children will attest that their energy and curiosity and capacity for action far exceeds that of adults.

> **When we are young, no task is too daunting.**

What happens to us then, as we grow older, and especially as we leave our homes and families and venture out into the world of Public life? We meet resistance. Part of that resistance is physical: The tasks get greater; the obstacles are bigger than we thought; we tire more easily. The physical world is there, constantly pushing back on us. The philosopher Maurice Merleau-Ponty called it "the flesh of the world," the "primordial stuff in which we all inhere and which is the ultimate ground of all human experience." In other words, we would not exist without the physical world.

★★★★

The second part of the equation for power is "distance." We don't exert force on the world just for the sake of tiring ourselves out. We want to "move it" someplace, in one direction or another. In the social world, that means we are trying to move the world-as-it-is to become a different place, the world-as-it-could-be. Where does this "could-be world" come from? It comes from our imaginations, from our souls, from our hearts, from our guts. If we are truly born in the "image and likeness" of God, then it is the divine spirit within us that constantly seeks to create the world in a new way. In order to do so, however, we must exert power on the real world, which is force times distance, divided by time. So the further we want to move the world, the more force we need to exert.

> **This "could-be world" comes from our imaginations, from our souls, from our hearts, from our guts.**

★ ★ ★ ★

The other factor of power in the physicists' definition of action, of course, is "time." Despite what Einstein and others might say, time is real, at least for human beings. It is real because we all die. There is no getting around this fact, and the older you get, the more you realize and accept it. We are on the earth for a limited number of years. Some of us live to the "ripe" old age of 80 or 90. Some of us die too young: at birth or in our teen years or as a young adult or right before we retire. But we all die, which means that we have limited time in which to act. How we use the time we have is what matters in terms of how much power we exercise in our lifetime.

> **We all die, which means that we have limited time in which to act.**

★★★★

To act is what it means to be human. When we stop acting we are dead. Action is what keeps the human race alive. We come out of the womb ready to act. If we don't start squealing right away, the parent or midwife or doctor or nurse will give us a quick smack on the bottom to get us breathing.

We are placed on our mother's breast, and one of the first things we do is act to get fed, reaching for a breast we instinctively know will do the job. A little while later, we begin to make eye contact with our parents, beginning the process of communication with others that will last a lifetime.

Action is like oxygen. We can't exist without it. It is a basic human need. You know this from your own life. You need to eat, so you get up from your chair and find something to eat. You feel tired, so you crawl into bed. You get attracted by someone, so you go out on a date, hoping it might lead to more "action."

What happens when we don't act? We have a word for it. We say that people are "comatose" or "in a coma," which means they are totally unresponsive, unable to act, appearing to be dead. The way we know they are out of the coma is that they act, even if it is something as small as blinking their eyelids.

People are pretty aware of this need to act in private life. If people we know becomes lethargic, drawing into themselves, shutting down, we tell them they need to get themselves together and "do" something…anything really.

"Pull yourself together," we'll say. Or, "You've got to exert yourself more." Or, "Let's go for a walk or out to dinner." The ultimate act of non-action is suicide, because it takes away any possibility of additional action, at least on this side of death.

★★★★

Action is even more critical in Public life, but it is also easier to avoid. We can go through life without acting publicly much at all. When I was a kid I was taught to "go to church, say your prayers, obey your parents and teachers." Those seemed to be the only criteria for success that my parents cared about. I had to learn to act in the Public arena. Perhaps we all do, but I do know that action is our natural instinct and we often repress it because of our education and upbringing.

Why don't people act more often in Public life? If action is a natural drive, why do people avoid it? This question has always fascinated me. I know it is not because people are "apathetic," that is, "not-caring or not-feeling." Scratch the surface even a little with most people and you find that they care very much about themselves, about others, and about the world. In organizing we talk about "agitating" people, and what we mean is to get them to think about what they already care about.

> **Action is more critical in Public life, but it is also easier to avoid.**

Human beings do care. That is what makes us human. We are not unfeeling automatons. We are genetically programmed to act. Yet often we do not. Why?

The biggest reason is that our culture and education system teaches us not to. Or at least it fails to teach us *to act* and *how to act*.

Let's look at elementary and high school. What are the biggest values we are taught: not to question why things are the way they are, not to question assumptions and stereotypes, not to be our own person. We are taught not to cause any trouble, not to ask too many questions, not to be "different" from all the other students. We get "check marks" on our report cards for "fails to listen to directions" or "disruptive in class."

By the time some of us get to college, the lesson

has become clear: If you want to get straight A's, then learn to regurgitate what the professor taught in class, preferably in the form and language the professor prefers. Unless you go to a great college or university, you are not encouraged to challenge the status quo, to think originally, and certainly not to "act out" as they say.

★★★★

I was thrown out of a Catholic seminary. I'm not ashamed of it, because I did nothing wrong. All I did was study philosophers and theologians who were not "approved" and try to engage my professors and fellow seminarians about these new ideas instead of just repeating the traditional scholastic philosophy we were being taught. (They actually pulled me out of line at our "tonsure" ceremony and the bishop told me that I was being dismissed for being too much of a "troublemaker.")

★★★★

It is these kinds of experiences that teach people they need to "go along to get along." This makes them afraid to act, because they don't want to pay a price for their actions. And so they begin to be afraid of "rocking the boat" and eventually they make this part of their personality. What's worse, they then pass that same trait on to their children, continuing the cycle.

Our culture then reinforces this tendency against action in Public life. What is television if not an outlet for passivity? According to the A.C. Nielsen Co., the average American watches more than 4 hours of TV each day (or 28 hours/week, or 2 months of nonstop TV-watching per year). In a 65-year life, that person will have spent 9 years glued to the tube. Not only does the amount of time spent militate against action, what people *watch* does as well. A "reality" show, for example, is the ultimate in phony action: We watch other people doing things, rather than doing them ourselves. That is also true of sports. We'd rather watch baseball on TV rather than go outside and toss a ball with our kids or even go to a ballgame ourselves. And politics becomes a spectator sport on TV. We get daily polls and colored state maps right up until Election Day, rather than getting out and campaigning door-to-door for the candidate of our choice.

> **Our culture reinforces this tendency against action in Public life.**

What gets destroyed in all this is our sense of initiative and responsibility. We end up wanting to blame someone else for the state of the world (the "crooked politicians," the "media," the "special interests"). Or we delegate our right to act to others who tell us what to do and when to do it. As good as the 2008 Obama campaign was in recruiting people to act in the political process, for example, it still remains a top-down, "we'll tell you what is important" and "you support our agenda" movement.

★★★★

Another reason people don't act is that we don't have *mentors* and *heroes* anymore. We get *celebrities*. The difference between a mentor/hero and a celebrity is that the first encourages us to act and the second acts in our stead. So we have entire magazines (*People, National Enquirer*) and television shows (*Entertainment Tonight*) that give us our fill of what our celebrities did today. This partially fills our need to act ourselves. We watch sports on TV to see how our "heroes" act after they make a touchdown, and somehow we feel that we have done an end-zone dance as well.

Real heroes challenge us to act ourselves. "Ask not what your country can do for you," John F. Kennedy said, "ask what you can do for your country." Mother Teresa, Dorothy Day, Mother Jones, Susan B. Anthony all urged us to get out and do something ourselves, not applaud what *they* were doing. Who are the mentors and heroes in your life? If you can't name many, then you probably aren't going to act very much in Public life. If you do have some, they probably are what makes you want to get out and do something to make the world a better place.

> **Real heroes challenge us to act ourselves.**

★★★★

My mother graduated from Grinnell College in Iowa at a time when few women did so. She met my father, an Irish national, when she picked him up hitchhiking. She raised a family of children, dealt with an alcoholic husband, and instilled in me the need to act.

My other role model was my sister Mary, who was the only one to support my desire to travel to Europe during college. Mary had her own family, but like my other brothers and sisters she never left Iowa. I think she knew that I was going for both of us.

It is not surprising that these two women would have taught me about action, because mothers take action instinctively to protect their family and to raise their children. Fathers do as well, of course, but some—like mine—are content to leave the child-rearing to their wives. But women know they have to act for the family to survive, and they are the ones who eventually have to push their babies out of the nest if they are to learn to survive on their own.

The final reason people don't act is that they either like things the way they are or don't know how to act effectively. About the first reason, there is not much anyone can do. If you like things the way they are, you are either very rich and don't care about other people or you just don't know what is going on in the world.

If you don't know how to act effectively, then there is great hope for you. This is actually what organizing is all about: teaching people how to act effectively. We even have a word for it: power. Power is simply the ability to act effectively with others on the *world-as-it-is* in order to make it more like the *world-as-it-could-be*. That is why we need organization. I spend more time in this booklet and in others in this series on power and how to get it, but the important thing now is to realize that in order to exercise power you need to interact with others and together take action on the rest of the world. This will cause an inevitable reaction, which will lead to your next action.

But first, we need to talk about why we act, or more specifically about what we get out of action in Public life. The reason to act in Public life is that it fulfills us as human beings. We are genetically programmed to act. We want to act. We need to act. If you don't believe me, just watch how young children operate. Babies and toddlers are constantly acting on their surroundings, including on their parents, and it is this action that allows them to grow and develop, even before they have any cognitive function whatsoever.

We grow and develop and gain wisdom through action, not by thinking about acting. That is why in good citizen organizations, every Public action is followed by an *evaluation*: because we don't want to lose the opportunity that the action has provided to learn. We want to know what we did right and what we did wrong. How did the opposition react and how did we respond in turn? What would we do differently in the future? What are our next steps? Without action, there can be no evaluation; and without evaluation, there can be no insight or growth.

> **We grow and develop and gain wisdom through action, not by thinking about acting.**

We act because it is human to act. We are curious animals; we want to know the "why" of things and especially the "why not" of things. We want to be part of life, to make a difference, to contribute something, to be relevant. We want to show our children how to be strong, how to stand up to the bully, how to make the world a better place.

We act because we have a conscience that will not allow us to sit idly by while things aren't right. We experience anger when we observe injustice and want to help do something to stop it. We have a vision of how the world could be, and we want to make it happen. We are "could be" people, who see the world as it could be, who see the potential in people, who are created and aimed at doing something to make things happen, who believe in ourselves rather than in what our social upbringing tries to make us into.

During the Korean War, the U.S. government was drafting young men to fight in the army. When I was kicked out of the seminary, the draft board was immediately informed and I was classified "1A," which meant I would soon be killing people in a uniform with the blessing of both my government and my church.

However, I sent the draft board a letter informing them that I was a conscientious objector. At my hearing I was informed that Catholics were not allowed to be conscientious objectors. They even got a letter from the pastor of my parents' church stating that I was not and could not be a conscientious objector.

I was prepared to go to Leavenworth prison (at a time when conscientious objectors were persecuted by the other prisoners), but I received a reprieve when I turned twenty-six and was no longer eligible for the draft. It was then that I decided I had to go to New York and learn how to organize to change the world-as-it-is into more like the world-as-I-knew-it-could-be.

What do we get out of acting on the world in conjunction with others? We get a feeling of power and dignity and self-worth. We sleep better at night. We can look our loved ones in the eye. We feel respect from our families and neighbors and friends and even our opponents. "I am somebody," Jesse Jackson teaches people to chant, but they become somebody by acting, not chanting.

If we don't learn to act in Public life, we become a follower. Now, there are a lot of followers: What would leaders be without them? I estimate that 75-80% of all people are, and will remain, followers. Following is a lot easier than leading, because leading necessitates entering into the unknown, and we are all afraid of the unknown. But some people are not satisfied to be leaders. They don't want to wait around for someone else to tell them what to do. They want to act on their own. They want to be in charge of their own life.

What the Industrial Areas Foundation (IAF) really has done over the past 70 years is provide a place where people can have the experiences they need to become effective leaders. Our local organizations are "leadership universities" where people who want to become leaders in Public life can learn to do so. It is not "natural" to be a leader, nor are most leaders "naturals." They are people who want to act and are able to transcend their background, limitations, upbringing (and often formal schooling) in order to learn to lead. In order to do that, they need opportunities and mentors.

> **Our local organizations
> are "leadership universities"
> where people who want to become
> leaders in Public life can learn to do so.**

★ ★ ★ ★

One of my first Public actions was as a paperboy in rural Iowa. I started out at age eleven delivering papers, but by the time I was fifteen I was promoted to disbursing the correct amount of papers to the other carriers, including some much older than I was. If one of the delivery people didn't show on a particular day, it was my responsibility to do whatever it took to get those papers to the customers that day.

Years later, when I needed to "borrow" $600 to go to Europe, I knew there was only one person I could ask. It was my mentor at the newspaper, editor Tom Welch, to whom I went, because I knew that he would understand my need to see the world. After all, he was the one who had mentored me in my job. He was the one who had taught me to be curious, to take risks, to have a sense of adventure, to have a vision of the world. He knew, as well as I did, that I needed to get out of Iowa, and he put his money where his mouth was. I don't think he thought for one minute that he would get his money back, and he never did. But he knew he was my mentor, and that's what mentors do.

There is one more thing we get out of acting in Public life: It is fun. The worst thing a person can be is bored. Take my word for it. Boredom is the antithesis of action, and when we are bored we are less than human. Human beings are meant to be engaged in life. We are made in the image and likeness of God, and God got bored, so he acted: He created the universe. Not bad for six days' work.

> **Human beings are meant to be engaged in life.**

Of course, God made a mistake at first. He tried to organize creation around universals: everyone the same kind, everyone following the same rules, everyone with the same values. It blew up on him. Adam and Eve ate the fruit of the one tree they were forbidden to eat. Their first two boys couldn't get along, so Cain killed Able.

Eventually, the humans started to build the Tower of Babel, so that they could reach the sky and presumably they would become gods. But God had enough of this nonsense and decided to start over again, this time with diversity instead of unity. Everyone would have a different language; people would look, act, and think differently; and there would be many gods. Then God would chose one of those people—the weakest one, of course—and start all over again.

That is the Jewish view of the world, as articulated by Rabbi Jonathan Sacks in his book *The Dignity of Difference*. In his view, the world is physical, concrete, and constantly changing. So when we act, we don't know exactly what is going to happen. The implications of his analysis are many, but one of them is that our diversity creates action. Because people are different from one another and because the world is full of specificity and particularity, not universals, people are forced to act with one another, and that reaction leads to inevitable reaction. In fact, the purpose of action is relationship and reaction.

★★★★

Action always involves risk. Initiating a phone call, for example, is quite different than answering a phone call. We have to get out of our comfort zones to act, because we never really know how things are going to turn out. If we're honest we admit that sometimes we make things worse by our actions. But that doesn't mean we don't act. It means that we have to learn how to act more effectively.

> **Action always involves risk.**

Most people, if and when they begin acting in Public life, spend a lot of time flailing around, wasting a lot of time and effort on actions that turn out to be quite ineffective. They are influenced by other people, who tell them not to "rock the boat." Or, when they aren't immediately successful or hit the first little bump, they give up. What they lack is a compelling vision of what could be. They also fail to understand that their action will always be influenced by how others react to their action.

In organizing, we have a phrase for this. We say, "The action is in the inevitable reaction." What we mean is that we do not know exactly what will happen when we act. All we know is that when we act there inevitably will be a reaction to which we, in turn, must respond.

What do I mean by "the action is in the reaction"? I mean that it is not so important what *we* do as what the other person does or how the physical world pushes back at us. Our action sets their reaction in motion, and then it is our job to use that reaction to take our next action. I'll give you a simple example.

★★★★

In Chicago, one of the organizations affiliated with the Industrial Areas Foundation (IAF) is called United Power for Action and Justice. When then Lt. Governor Pat Quinn was named governor after his predecessor, Rob Blagojevich, was arrested and indicted for corruption, the organization immediately asked for a sit-down with Quinn. That was the action.

At the meeting the delegation went through a list of things they wanted the new governor to do. He agreed to some, said he would get back to them on others. At the end of the meeting, however, Quinn said, "Now, there is one thing I want from you." The group listened intently, because they knew that this would be the true "reaction" to their "action."

"I need you to organize a large, grassroots meeting within thirty days, where I can come and talk directly to

the people of the state about all that needs to be done," the new governor said. The meeting then ended, with the United Power delegation saying that they would get back to Quinn in three days with an answer to his request. What they were doing is buying some time to analyze his reaction and then act on it, one way or the other.

The result was that the organization held two meetings with Quinn within the next two months, each with over 800 people. This did two things:

1. *It solidified the organization's relationship with the new governor. It raised the recognition of the organization with both the media and other organizations in the state.*

2. *It exercised the organization's internal networks, teaching them how to turn out troops on short notice in response to the reaction of someone in power that needed their help.*

How do we act effectively with others on the physical world? This is not an easy question, nor is the answer simple or obvious. It is clear that we are not meant to act alone. In fact, in organizing we have a word for this. We call it "symbolic protest." It is the image of a single person or small group carrying placards outside a meeting of powerful people who are making decisions that affect the world greatly. Inside the meeting, there is no recognition—much less concern for—the protest going on outside. In fact, if the powerless protest turns violent, the power people simply have the protestors removed by the police, which they, of course, control.

So, acting on our own and in isolation is neither effective nor threatening to those in power. And one of the universals of action in Public life is that there is no change without some sort of pressure or threat. What is threatening to people in power are two things: organized people and organized money. Those are the two elements that will get the attention of people in power and force them to react. And when they inevitably do, then their reaction forces us to act in response.

> **Acting on our own and in isolation is neither effective nor threatening to those in power.**

★★★★

But how do we get ourselves—and others—to act together? In one of the other books in this series, *The Power of Relational Action*, I describe the method that I helped develop over the years of conducting what the IAF calls "one-to-ones" or "relational meetings." The purpose of conducting hundreds or even thousands of these short, focused, relational meetings is simply to see *if you and the other person have enough in common to* act together in Public life. Many of the people you meet, you will discover, have little in common with you. They like the world-as-it-is, or at least they have no interest in trying to change it. Those are the people you get away from as quickly as possible.

But there are others, maybe three or four in every ten you meet, who share many of the values and passions and what we call "self-interests" that you have. These are people with whom you can go into action. Maybe not right away, and maybe not in a big way initially, but as the trust and relationship between you grow you will discover that you have a "kindred soul," someone who shares at least part of your vision for the world-as-it-could-be.

There are times when you have to challenge—what we organizers call "agitate"—people to get them to act. But it is really they who are challenging and agitating themselves. You are just providing the kindling to get them started. And many times you will find that they are challenging and agitating you as well. It is this dynamic that leads to action.

> **There are times when you have to challenge people to get them to act.**

★★★★

Finally, you will find that as you get into action in the world-as-it-is, with people who share your passions and self-interests, you will realize that you need to *organize*. That is, you will need to build an organization that can help you do your action-in-the-world. Action leads to organization. Not in a bureaucratic way, but in an organic way.

The purpose of organization is power. That is why people build them, and that is why those in power are afraid of them. There is nothing more terrifying to the power structure than organized people, especially if they also learn how to organize their money and other resources. What you will find is that action in Public life leads to organization, because organization is the only way to get meaningful power. For, as the physicists say, power is force times distance, divided by time.

> **The purpose of organization is power.**

★★★★

In a further book, I intend to reflect on organization and power, but here I want to finish my thoughts about action in Public life with a list of "universals":

1. We act because we are beings. Being triggers action.

2. We act together because we need each other in order to succeed. We are relational beings.

3. All action results in an inevitable reaction. We use that reaction to take our next action.

4. The two most feared things by those in power are organized people and organized money. Put the two together and you have real power.

5. Action is to an organization as oxygen is to the body. It cannot live without it.

6. The "relational action"—the one-to-one meeting between two people trying to decide if they should get into action together—is the most powerful weapon we human beings have.

7. It is not "I think, therefore I am." Rather, it is "I am, therefore I act."

8. Diversity creates action. That is why, when we act, we do not know what is going to happen. It depends on others, on the world, and on ourselves.

9. Everyone acts in his or her perceived self-interest.

10. We need to act in order to participate fully in Public life and thus become fully human.

OTHER RESOURCES ON ORGANIZING

THE POWER OF RELATIONAL ACTION
by Edward T. Chambers

Ed Chambers mulls about the building of relationships in public life that allow us to share our values, passions and interests with one another—what he calls "mixing human spirits." He describes the art of the relational meeting or "one-to-one," which he helped developed and which is now being used by clergy, leaders and organizers around the United States and in several other countries to build their congregations and community institutions and to take joint action for the common good.
33-page paperback, $5.95

THE BODY TRUMPS THE BRAIN
by Edward T. Chambers

The executive director of the Industrial Areas Foundation (IAF) looks at how humans learn with all their senses—including instinct and intuition—and how our educations system tries to downplay what he calls "social knowledge" in favor of academic exercises.
48-page paperback, $5.95

BEING TRIGGERS ACTION
Organizing for Power, Action and Justice
by Edward T. Chambers

Ed Chambers mulls about the nature of being itself and how being "triggers" action in the world. He explores the "inter"-action between our self, other selfs, and the world, because it is in that interaction where being takes place.
38 pages, paperback, $5.95

AVAILABLE FROM BOOKSELLERS OR CALL 800-397-2282
WWW.ACTAPUBLICATIONS.COM

OTHER RESOURCES ON ORGANIZING

ROOTS FOR RADICALS
by Edward T. Chambers

Ed Chambers' description of the "universals" of organizing. Demonstrates how to make connections across differences of nationality, culture and class. Offers practical ideas and examples for the development of citizen and congregational power.
152-pages hardcover, $12.95

EFFECTIVE ORGANIZING
FOR CONGREGATIONAL RENEWAL
by Michael Gecan

The author of *Going Public* and one of the directors of the Metro Industrial Areas Foundation describes how the tools of organizing can and are transforming Protestant, Catholic, Jewish and Muslim congregations. Included are five case studies of congregations that have used this process to grow.
54 pages, paperback, $5.95

AFTER AMERICA'S MIDLIFE CRISIS
by Michael Gecan

Michael Gecan paints a vivid picture of civic, political, and religious institutions in decline, from suburban budget crises to failing public schools, what he describes as "a national midlife crisis." He shows how local organizational efforts can create vibrant institutions that truly serve their constituents and preserve and advance their communities.
128-page hardcover, $14.95

AVAILABLE FROM BOOKSELLERS OR CALL 800-397-2282
WWW.ACTAPUBLICATIONS.COM